# THE CHILDREN'S BIBLE

## Volume 11

**A Golden Press / Funk & Wagnalls, Inc. Book**

Published by Western Publishing Company, Inc.

Distributed by Funk & Wagnalls, Inc. New York

Library of Congress Catalog Card Number: 81-81439

ISBN 0-8343-0048-6 (Volume 11)
ISBN 0-8343-0037-0 (12 Volume Set)

# CONTENTS

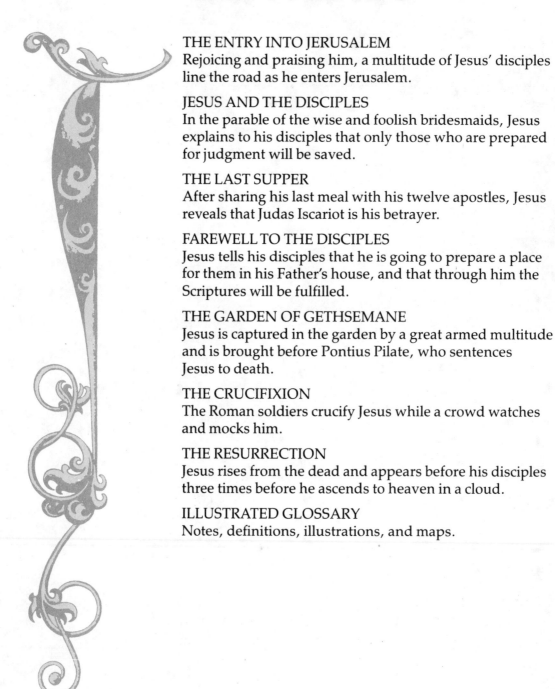

# INTRODUCTION

For the disciples, Jesus' death was the most unsettling event of their lives. At first they thought his crucifixion meant that all their hopes and dreams for a new life of love and peace were destroyed. They felt sad and lost. But then, the Gospels say, Jesus was raised from the dead and appeared before his disciples. He returned to them and assured them that his crucifixion was part of God's plan to bring all people into his Kingdom. Jesus' resurrection filled his disciples with a new and powerful hope. When other people who had not known Jesus began to ask about him, the disciples told them the story of his crucifixion and resurrection. They believed that these were the most important things for the people to know.

Before Jesus' resurrection, men and women were trapped by sin. It was as though they were being held hostage far away from God. Christians say that Jesus offered his life as a ransom for all men and women. He sacrificed his life to free them from death. If they believe in him, the Bible says, they will live with God in heaven forever. This is why Easter Sunday, the day when Christians celebrate the Resurrection, is such a happy day. Christians celebrate because they are free, free to love God and to be disciples of Jesus.

The story of the Passion, as Jesus' suffering and death are called, begins with his decision to go to Jerusalem. Jerusalem was a special place for the Jews. Because the temple was there, they believed that God had a special love for the city. Jesus wanted to preach to the people of this great city as he had preached in the small towns and the countryside of Galilee. Jesus went there to proclaim his message about God's Kingdom to the whole world and to free the people to love God.

This was an important and dangerous decision for Jesus. The Jewish and Roman leaders were afraid of him because they thought he wanted to lead the people in violent rebellion against the political and religious authorities. They were afraid that Jesus had come to Jerusalem to take over the city and begin his revolution there.

The Romans and many of the Jewish leaders never understood that Jesus was the Messiah of peace and obedient love. Jesus warned his disciples never to use violence. Even on the night he was arrested, Jesus did not allow his followers to defend him with their swords. This does not mean, of course, that Jesus never got angry. He was angry when he chased the moneychangers out of the temple. These men were selling ani-

mals for the temple sacrifice and were exchanging local coins for the money that Jews from other countries brought with them to Jerusalem. Even then, Jesus only picked up a whip to drive out the animals. He did not strike the men.

Jesus expected a great deal from his followers. He told his disciples to love and serve one another. He told them to love the poor, the hungry, and people in prison. And he told them that by doing this they would be loving and serving him too. He wanted them to love him by doing something for those who needed help. Jesus warned his followers that on the day of judgment he would return to ask them how they had lived.

Jesus told his disciples that he would be with them only a little longer and that he would be in heaven until the judgment day. He knew that his disciples would miss him, just as you miss a friend who has gone away. So during the last meal he shared with his apostles, Jesus told them they should always gather together as they were doing on that evening. He told them that when they met they should eat bread and drink wine, just as he was doing. Jesus gave his disciples a special gift: he promised them that when they did this in his name, he would come and join them. They would never have to be alone again. He would always be with them.

This special meal that Christians share to celebrate and remember Jesus' death and resurrection is called the Eucharist or Communion. Christians say that when they take the bread and wine that is served in their churches at the Eucharist, Jesus is with them. It is almost as though they were already in heaven with him. Like the Jews who remember the exodus during the feast of Passover, Christians remember that Jesus led them out of the bondage of sin.

Just as Jews say that God made a covenant with them on Sinai, Christians say that God offered the world a new covenant in Jesus. The Sinai covenant was celebrated and sealed by the blood of the lambs killed for the sacrifice. The new covenant was celebrated and made final by Jesus' sacrifice on the cross. And just as the Sinai covenant demanded that the people of Israel live their whole lives in obedience to God, so the new covenant demanded that Christians live as Jesus taught them.

After the meal with his disciples, Jesus went out to face his death. On the way, he stopped to pray in the Garden of Gethsemane. As he had told his followers to do, Jesus turned to God in a moment of fear. He asked God to spare him from the suffering he knew was waiting for him. Jesus was afraid just as any man or woman would have been afraid in his place, and he felt alone. But Jesus was also obedient to God. He was tempted by his fear, but he obeyed God. He knew that in order for the world to be given the new covenant, God's plan was that he suffer and die on the cross.

Jesus faced his death almost all alone. His apostles had fled from him in fear, and even Peter, who was strong and brave, denied that he knew Jesus. The only people who did not abandon Jesus were the apostle John and the women who had listened to Jesus as he taught in the towns and countryside. They alone had the courage to stand by him in that terrible hour.

After Jesus' death and resurrection, Peter himself told the story of his denial of Jesus. He wanted to warn people that all Christians, no matter how strong they think they are, may be tempted to turn away from Jesus. But Peter also told this story to comfort the men and women who heard him. For after he had denied Jesus, Peter wept and repented, and Jesus welcomed him back. Even though everyone will sin, Jesus promises forgiveness as long as the sinners repent and have faith.

Crucifixion was commonly used by the Romans only to kill slaves and rebels. It was a harsh punishment, and Jesus died a terrible and painful death on the cross. The soldiers were ready to throw Jesus' body into a common grave, as was the custom for victims of crucifixion, but a rich man named Joseph claimed the body and gave Jesus a proper burial in his family's tomb.

If the story of Jesus of Nazareth had ended here we would probably have never heard of this man, but Christians say that the story does not end here at all. Instead, God once again acted in the world, and for the world, by raising Jesus in glory from the dead. Christians say that this was God's most powerful act. Death had no power over Jesus. He was resurrected and returned to talk to his disciples. He told them that because he had conquered death, death would have no power over them either. He had conquered death for them.

For Christians, Jesus' resurrection was the beginning of the new world God had promised to men and women. Jesus rose up in glory from his tomb. Nothing in the world could ever be the same again after Jesus' resurrection; everything would be new and fresh. He invited all his followers to share in the glory of his resurrection, if they were willing to bear the cross with him by serving each other in obedience to God. According to Christians, on the day of Jesus' resurrection, the world woke up to a new and sunny morning that would never end.

# from the
# BOOKS OF
# MATTHEW, MARK,
# LUKE, and JOHN

# THE ENTRY INTO JERUSALEM

T came to pass that when Jesus was near Bethphage and Bethany, at the hill called the Mount of Olives, he sent forth two of his disciples, saying:

"Go into the village near by and upon entering you shall find a colt tied on which no man has ever sat. Loose him and bring him here. And if any man asks you, 'Why do you loose him?,' say to him, 'Because the Lord has need of him.'"

The two disciples went their way and found it as he had said to them. As they were loosing the colt, the owners said to them, "Why do you loose the colt?" And they said, "The Lord has need of him."

They brought him to Jesus and they laid their garments upon the colt, and they set Jesus upon it. And as he rode, they spread their clothes on the road.

When he had come near the slope of the Mount of Olives, the whole multitude of his disciples began to rejoice and praise God with a loud voice for all the mighty works that they had seen, saying, "Blessed be the king that comes in the name of the Lord. Peace in heaven, and glory in the highest."

Then some of the Pharisees from among the multitude said to him, "Master, rebuke your disciples."

He answered and said to them, "I tell you that if they should hold their peace, the stones would immediately cry out."

He had come near to the city, and when he saw it he wept over it, saying:

"If only you knew, in this day of yours, the things which concern your peace! But they are hid from your eyes. The days shall come that your enemies shall build a trench around you and keep you in on every side. They shall throw you to the ground and your children within you. They shall

not leave you one stone on another, because you did not acknowledge the time when God visited you."

And when he entered Jerusalem, all the city was moved, saying, "Who is this?" And the multitude said, "This is Jesus the prophet of Nazareth of Galilee."

653

## JESUS DRIVES OUT MONEYCHANGERS

Jesus went into the temple of God, and drove out all them that sold and bought in the temple, and overturned the tables of the moneychangers, and the seats of them that sold doves and said to them, "My house shall be called the house of prayer, but you have made it a den of thieves."

And the blind and the lame came to him in the temple and he healed them.

But when the chief priests and scribes saw the children crying in the temple and saying, "Hosanna to the son of David," they were much displeased.

They said to him, "Do you hear what they say?" Jesus answered saying, "Yes, have you never read, 'Out of the mouth of babes, O God, you have drawn perfect praise'?"

And he left them and went out of the city into Bethany, and he lodged there.

## THE FIG TREE WITHERS AWAY

On the next day, when they were coming from Bethany, Jesus was hungry. Seeing a fig tree far away that had leaves, he went to see whether he might find any fig on it. But when he came to it, he found nothing but leaves, for it was not yet the time for figs.

And he said to it, "Let no fruit grow on you from now and forever." And immediately the fig tree withered away.

When the disciples saw it, they marveled, saying, "How soon the fig tree has withered away!" Jesus answered and said to them, "Truly I say to you, you if you have faith and doubt not, shall not only do this which was done to the fig tree, but also if you say to this mountain, 'Be removed and be cast into the sea,' it shall be done. All things you ask in prayer, believing, you shall receive."

# THE GREEDY WORKMEN

When Jesus came into the temple, the chief priests and the elders of the people came to him as he was teaching, and said, "By what authority do you do these things, and who gave you this authority?"

Jesus would not answer their question, but he began to speak to them in parables, saying:

"A certain man planted a vineyard and hedged it round about and dug a wine press in it, and built a tower, and then let it out to workmen, and went to a distant land.

"When the time of harvest drew near, he sent his servants to the workmen to collect the fruits of the vineyard. But the workmen took his servants, and beat one, and killed another, and stoned another.

"Again he sent other servants, and they did likewise to them. Last of all he sent his son to them, saying, 'They will respect my son.'

"But when the workmen saw the son, they said among themselves, 'This is the heir. Come, let us kill him and let us seize his inheritance.'

"And they caught him, and threw him out of the vineyard, and killed him.

"When the lord of the vineyard comes, what will he do to those workmen?" Jesus asked.

They said to him:

"He will miserably destroy those wicked men, and will rent out his vineyard to other workmen, who will pay him his share of the fruit when they ripen."

When the chief priests and Pharisees had heard his parable, they knew that he spoke of them. But when they tried to lay their hands on him, they were afraid of the multitude because it took him for a prophet.

## GOD AND CAESAR

The Pharisees watched Jesus, and they sent forth spies who pretended to be honest men, that they might make use of his words to deliver him into the power and authority of the governor.

The spies questioned him, saying, "Master, we know that you are true and teach the truth, showing no favor, but truly teaching the way of God. Tell us therefore whether you think it is lawful for us to give tribute to Caesar or not?"

But he saw their craftiness and said to them, "Why do you try to trap me? Show me a coin. Whose name and image has it?"

They answered and said, "Caesar's." And he said to them, "Give therefore to Caesar the things which are Caesar's and to God the things which are God's."

And they could not twist his words before the people. They marveled at his answer, and held their peace.

## THE WIDOW'S PENNY

Jesus looked up and saw the rich men casting their gifts into the treasury. He saw also a certain poor widow casting in two pennies. And he said:

"Truly I say to you, that this poor widow has cast in more than all of them. For all these others have given offerings to God out of their abundance. But she in her poverty has given all she had to live upon."

## THE UNWORTHY GUEST

Jesus spoke to them again by a parable, saying:

"The kingdom of heaven is like a certain king who prepared a marriage for his son, and sent forth his servants to call them that were invited to the wedding. And they would not come.

"Again, he sent out other servants, saying, 'Tell them that are invited that I have prepared my dinner. My oxen and my fat cattle are killed and all things are ready. Tell them to come to the marriage.'

"But they made light of it, and went their ways, one to his farm, another to his merchandise. And the rest took his servants and treated them spitefully, and slew them.

"When the king heard of this, he was angry. He sent forth his armies and destroyed those murderers, and burnt up their city.

"Then he said to his servants, 'The wedding is ready, but those who were invited were not worthy. Go therefore into the highways, and as many as you shall find, invite them to the marriage.'

"So those servants went out into the highways and gathered together as many as they found, both bad and good, and the wedding was furnished with guests.

"When the king came in to see the guests, he saw a man among them who did not have on a wedding robe. And he said to him, 'Friend, how did you come in here not having a wedding robe?'

"The man answered nothing.

"Then the king said to his servants, 'Bind him hand and foot and take him away, and cast him into outer darkness.'

"There shall be weeping and gnashing of teeth. For many are called, but few are chosen."

# JESUS AND THE DISCIPLES

AS Jesus went out of the temple, one of his disciples said to him, "Look, Master, at these stones and these buildings!" He said, "As for these things which you see, the days shall come when there shall not be left one stone upon another that has not been thrown down."

And as he sat upon the Mount of Olives, his disciples came to him privately, saying, "Tell us. When shall these things be? And what shall be the sign of your coming and of the end of the world?"

And Jesus answered and said to them:

"Take care that no man deceives you. For many shall come in my name, saying, 'I am Christ,' and shall deceive many. You shall hear of wars and rumors of wars, but see that you do not become troubled, for all these things must come to pass. This is not the end yet.

"For nation shall rise against nation, and kingdom against kingdom. There shall be famines and pestilences and earthquakes in different places. All this is the beginning of sorrows.

"Then there shall be great troubles such as there have not been since the beginning of the world, troubles that there never have been and there never shall be. And unless those days were to be shortened, no living things could be saved. But for the sake of my chosen ones, those days shall be shortened.

## THE END OF TIME

"The sun shall be darkened, and the moon shall not give her light, and the stars shall fall from heaven, and the powers of the heavens shall be shaken.

"Then the sign of the Son of man shall appear in the heavens, and then shall all the tribes of the earth mourn. And they shall see the Son of man coming in the clouds of heaven with power and great glory. And he shall send his angels with a great sound of a trumpet, and they shall gather together his chosen ones from the four winds, from one end of heaven to the other.

"Now learn a lesson from the fig tree: When its branch is still tender and puts forth leaves, you know that summer is near. So likewise you, when you see all these things, know that it is near, even at the doors.

"Truly I say to you, this generation shall not pass until all these things are fulfilled. Heaven and earth shall pass away, but my words shall not pass away.

"No man knows the day and the hour, not even the angels of heaven, but my Father only. Watch therefore, for you do not know what hour your Lord will come. But know this, that if the man of the house had known what

time the thief would come, he would have watched and would not have allowed his house to be broken into.

"Therefore, be ready also. For at the time when you do not think it, the Son of man is coming. Blessed is the servant whom his lord shall find doing his duty when he comes. Truly I tell you, he shall make him ruler over his goods.

## THE WISE AND FOOLISH BRIDESMAIDS

"Thus the kingdom of heaven shall be like ten bridesmaids who took their lamps and went forth to meet the bridegroom. Five of them were wise and five were foolish.

"They that were foolish took their lamps but took no oil with them. The wise ones took oil in vessels with their lamps.

"As the bridegroom was late, they you. Go instead to them that sell, and buy for yourselves.'

"While they went to buy, the bridegroom came and they that were ready went in with him to the marriage, and the door was shut. Afterwards the other bridesmaids came, saying, 'Lord, Lord, open the door to us.' But he answered and said, 'Truly, I do not know you.'

"Watch therefore, for you know neither the day nor the hour in which the Son of man comes.

all slumbered and slept. But at midnight the cry went up, 'Behold, the bridegroom comes. Go out to meet him.' Then all the bridesmaids rose up and trimmed their lamps. And the foolish said to the wise, 'Give us some of your oil, for our lamps have gone out.' But the wise answered, saying, 'We cannot, lest there should not be enough both for us and for

## THE UNPROFITABLE SERVANT

"Again the kingdom of heaven is like a man setting off for a distant country who called together his servants and delivered to them his goods. To one he gave five talents, to another two, and to another one—to each according to his special abilities. Then he set off on his journey.

"He who received the five talents went and traded with them and made five more. And likewise he who received two gained two more. But he who received one went and dug in the earth and hid his lord's money.

"After a long time, the lord of those servants came home and reckoned with them. He who had received five talents came and brought five more, saying, 'Lord, you gave me five talents. Behold, I have earned five more beside them.'

"His lord said to him, 'Well done, good and faithful servant. You have been faithful over a few things, I will make you ruler over many things. Come, share with your lord his joy.'

"Then he who had received the one talent came and said, 'Lord, I knew that you are a hard man harvesting where you have not sown, and gathering where you have not threshed. And I was afraid, and went and hid your money in the earth. Lo, here you have what is yours.'

"His lord said to him, 'Well done, good and faithful servant. You have been faithful over a few things, I will make you ruler over many things. Come share with your lord in his good fortune.'

"Then he who had received two talents came and said, 'Lord, you gave me two talents. Behold, I have earned two more beside them.'

"His lord answered and said to him, 'You wicked and lazy servant! You knew that I reap where I have not sown, and gather where I have not threshed. Therefore you should have loaned out my money and then at my returning I should have had my money back with interest.'

"Therefore take the talent from him, and give it to him who has ten talents. For to every one who has, more shall be given, and he shall have plenty. But from him who has not, shall be taken away even that which he has. Now cast the unprofitable servant into outer darkness.

"There shall be weeping and gnashing of teeth.

## THE DAY OF JUDGMENT

"When the Son of man shall come in his glory, and all the holy angels with him, then shall he sit upon his glorious throne, and before him shall be gathered all nations. And he shall separate them one from another, as a shepherd divides his sheep from the goats. He shall set the sheep on his right hand, but the goats on the left.

"Then the King shall say to those on his right hand, 'Come, you blessed of my Father, inherit the kingdom prepared for you from the beginning of the world. For I was hungry, and you gave me food. I was thirsty and you gave me drink. I was a stranger, and you took me in. I was naked and you clothed me. I was sick and you visited me. I was in prison and you came to me.'

"Then shall the righteous answer him, saying, 'Lord, when did we see you hungry, and feed you? Or thirsty, and give you drink? When did we see you a stranger, and take you in? Or naked, and clothe you? Or when did we see you sick, or in prison, and come to you?'

"And the King shall answer and say to them, 'Truly I tell you, inasmuch as you have done it to one of the least of these my brothers, you have done it to me.'

"Then he shall also say to those on his left hand, 'Be off, you accursed ones, into everlasting fire, prepared for the devil and his angels. For I was hungry and you did not feed me,

thirsty and you gave me nothing to drink. I was a stranger and you did not take me in. I was naked and you did not clothe me. I was sick and in prison and you did not visit me.'

"Then they too will answer him, saying, 'Lord, when did we see you hungry, or thirsty, or a stranger, or naked, or sick, or in prison, and did not help you?'

"Then shall he answer them saying, 'Truly I say to you, inasmuch as you did not do it to one of the least of these my brothers, you did not do it to me.'

"And these shall go away into eternal punishment, but the righteous into eternal life."

## JUDAS PLOTS TO BETRAY JESUS

And it came to pass when Jesus had finished all these sayings, that he said to his disciples, "You know that after two days is the feast of the Passover and the Son of man is to be betrayed and crucified."

Then the chief priests and the scribes and the elders of the people assembled together in the palace of the high priest, who was called Caiaphas. And they discussed how they might take Jesus by trickery and kill him.

But they said:

"Not on the feast day, lest there be an uproar among the people."

Then one of the twelve, called Judas Iscariot, went to the chief priests and said to them:

"What will you give me, if I deliver him to you?"

And when the chief priests heard him, they were glad and made an agreement with him for thirty pieces of silver. Judas accepted and from that time on he sought above all an occasion when the crowd would be absent.

# THE LAST SUPPER

On the day of unleavened bread, when the Passover lamb was to be sacrificed, Jesus sent forth two of his disciples, saying, "Go into the city and prepare the Passover feast, so that we may eat."

And the two disciples asked him: "Where are we to prepare it?"

He said, "When you have come into

the city, you will meet a man carrying a pitcher of water. Follow him into the house he enters. And say to the man of the house, 'The Master says, "Where is the guest chamber where I shall eat the Passover feast with my disciples?"' And he will show you a large room, furnished. Make ready there."

They went and found it all as he had told them, and they prepared the Passover feast.

When the evening came, Jesus sat down with the twelve. And he said to them, "How greatly I have desired to eat this Passover with you before I suffer. For I tell you, I will not eat another until it is fulfilled in the kingdom of God."

And as they were eating, Jesus took bread and blessed it, and breaking it into pieces he gave it to them, saying, "Take, eat; this is my body which is given for you. Do this in remembrance of me."

After supper he took the cup and when he had given thanks, he gave it to them saying:

"Drink you all of it; for this is the new testament in my blood, which is shed for you and for many, for the forgiveness of sins. Take this, and divide it among you. For I say to you, I will not drink of the fruit of the vine until I drink it anew with you in my Father's kingdom."

When the supper was ended, Jesus rose from the table, laid aside his garments, and took and fastened a towel about him. Pouring water into a basin he began to wash the disciples' feet and to wipe them with the towel he had wrapped around him.

When he came to Simon Peter, Peter said to him, "Lord, do you wash my feet?"

Jesus answered and said to him, "What I am doing you do not understand now, but you will understand after."

Peter said to him, "You shall never wash my feet."

Jesus answered him, saying, "If I do not wash you, you have no part with me."

Then Peter said to him, "Lord, not my feet only, but also my hands and

my head." But Jesus answered and said, "He who is clean needs only to wash his feet to be clean all over. And you are clean—but not all of you." Jesus added the words "not all of you" for he knew who was to betray him.

## "DO AS I HAVE DONE TO YOU"

After he had washed their feet and had taken his garments and was seated again, he said to them, "Do you know what I have done to you? You call me Master and Lord, and you speak well, for so I am. If I then, your Lord and Master, have washed your

feet, you also ought to wash one another's feet. For I have given you an example, that you should do as I have done to you.

"Truly, truly I say to you, the servant is not greater than his lord, nor is he that is sent greater than he that sent him. If you know these things, happy are you if you do them.

## JESUS REVEALS HIS BETRAYER

"I speak not of you all. I know whom I have chosen, for the scripture must be fulfilled which says,

'*He who eats bread with me*
*Has lifted up his heel against me.*' "

When Jesus had spoken, he was deeply troubled and said: "Truly, truly I say to you that one of you shall betray me."

Then the disciples looked at one another, not knowing of whom he spoke. Now close beside Jesus at the table was one of the disciples whom he loved. Simon Peter therefore beckoned to this disciple that he should ask who it was of whom Jesus spoke. Then he, leaning towards Jesus, said to him. "Lord, who is it?"

Jesus answered, "It is he to whom I shall give a piece of bread, when I have dipped it in the bowl." And when he had dipped the bread, he gave it to Judas Iscariot, the son of Simon.

And after Judas took the bread, Satan entered into him. Then Jesus said to him, "What you must do, do quickly."

Now no one at the table knew why he said this to him. For some of them thought, since Judas had the purse, that Jesus had told him to buy the things that would be needed for the festival, or that he should give something to the poor.

Then having received the bread, Judas went out immediately. And it was night.

# FAREWELL TO THE DISCIPLES

WHEN Judas had departed, Jesus said, "My children, for only a little while longer shall I be with you. You shall seek me, but as I said to the Jews, now I say to you: Where I am going, you cannot come.

"I give you a new commandment, that you love one another. As I have loved you, so also should you love one another. By this all people will know that you are my disciples, if you have love for one another.

"Greater love has no man than this: that a man lay down his life for his friends. You are my friends, if you do whatever I command you. I shall call you no longer servants, for a servant does not know what his lord does; but I have called you friends, for all that I have heard from my Father I have made known to you.

"Do not let your hearts be troubled. You believe in God; believe in me too. In my Father's house are many mansions. If it were not so, I would have told you. I go to prepare a place for you. And if I go and prepare a place for you, I will come again and take you back with me: that where I am, you may be also."

Simon Peter said to him, "Lord, where are you going?"

Jesus answered him, "Where I am going, you cannot follow me now, but you shall follow me later."

Peter said to him, "Lord, why cannot I follow you now? I would lay down my life for your sake."

Jesus answered him, "Will you lay down your life for my sake? Truly I say to you, the cock will not crow before you have denied me three times."

And he said to them, "When I sent you out without purses or shoes, did you lack anything?"

They said, "Nothing."

Then he said to them, "But now, he who has a purse, let him take it, and also his wallet. And he who has no sword, let him sell his robe and buy one. For I tell you, the writing in the scripture must be fulfilled in me: 'And he was counted among the outlaws.' For there is a purpose to things concerning me."

And they said, "Lord, see, here are two swords."

And he said to them, "It is enough."

# THE GARDEN OF GETHSEMANE

WHEN they had sung a hymn, they went out of the city to the Mount of Olives. Then Jesus said to them, "You will all desert me this night. For it is written, 'I will smite the shepherd, and the sheep of the flock will be scattered.' But after I have risen again, I will go before you into Galilee."

Peter answered and said to him, "Though everyone else may desert you, I will never desert you." Jesus said to him again, "I tell you truly that tonight before the cock crows, you shall deny me three times."

But Peter said to him, "Even though I should die with you, I would never deny you." And all the disciples said likewise.

Then Jesus went forth with them to a place over the brook Cedron, where there was a garden called Gethsemane. And he said to his disciples, "Sit here while I go over yonder and pray."

He took with him Peter and the two sons of Zebedee, and he began to be sorrowful and heavy of heart. Then he said to them, "My soul is exceeding sorrowful, even unto death. Stay you here and watch with me."

## JESUS PRAYS

He went on a little farther and fell to his face and prayed, saying, "O my Father, if it is possible, let this cup pass from me. Nevertheless, let not my will but your will be done."

And there appeared to him an angel from heaven, strengthening him. Then, being in agony, he prayed more earnestly, and his sweat was like great drops of blood falling to the ground.

And he came back to the disciples and found them asleep, and said to Peter, "What, could you not watch with me one hour? Watch now, and pray that you do not fall into temptation. The spirit is indeed willing, but the flesh is weak."

He went away again a second time and prayed, saying, "O Father, if this cup of suffering cannot pass from me unless I drink it, your will shall be done." And he came and found them asleep again, for their eyes were heavy. Then he left them and went away again and prayed a third time, saying the same words.

And when he returned, he found them asleep again, and he said to them, "Sleep on now and take your rest. It is enough. The hour has come when the Son of man shall be betrayed into the hands of sinners."

Then he said, "Rise up. Let us go Behold he that betrays me is at hand."

## THE BETRAYAL

While he was still speaking, Judas. one of the twelve, came, and with him a great multitude with swords and clubs, from the chief priests and the elders of the people.

Now he that betrayed him gave them a signal, saying, "Whomever I shall kiss, he is the one. Hold him fast."

And with that he came to Jesus and said, "Hail, Master," and kissed him.

Jesus said to him, "Friend, why have you come?" Then they came and laid hands on Jesus and took him.

Simon Peter, having a sword, drew it and struck the high priest's servant, and cut off his right ear. But Jesus said to him, "Put up your sword again in its place. For all who draw the sword shall die by the sword. Do you think that I could not now pray to my Father and he would immediately give me more than twelve legions of angels? But how then would the scriptures be fulfilled which say that it must be thus?" And he touched the man's ear and healed him.

At the same time he said to the multitudes, "Have you come out as if against a thief, with swords and clubs, to take me? I sat daily with you, teaching in the temple, and you laid not a hand on me."

But all this was done that the scriptures of the prophets might be fulfilled. Then all the disciples forsook him, and fled.

## PETER DENIES JESUS

They who had arrested Jesus led him to Caiaphas, the high priest, where the scribes and elders were assembled. But Peter followed him at a distance to the high priest's palace, and went in and sat with the servants, to see the end.

Now the chief priests and elders and all the council sought false witnesses against Jesus, so that they could put him to death. But they found nothing. Although many people came to testify falsely, still they found nothing.

At last two false witnesses came and said, "This fellow said, 'I am able to destroy the temple of God and to build it again in three days.' "

The high priest arose and said to him, "Do you answer nothing? What is it that these witnesses say against you?"

But Jesus held his peace. Then the high priest said to him, "I ask you by the living God that you tell us whether you are the Christ, the Son of God."

Jesus said to him, "You have said so. But I say to you: In the days to come, you shall see the Son of man sitting on the right hand of Power, and coming on the clouds of heaven."

Then the high priest tore his clothes, saying, "He has spoken blasphemy. What further need have we of witnesses? Behold, now you have heard his blasphemy. What think you?"

They answered and said, "He deserves to die."

Then they did spit in his face, and strike him, while others hit him with the palms of their hands, saying, "Prophesy to us, you Christ! Who is it that struck you?"

Simon Peter meanwhile remained outside with the servants. And the maid at the door said to him, "Are you not one of this man's disciples?"

And he said, "I am not."

The servants and officers had made a fire of coals for it was cold and they were standing by it, warming themselves. Peter stood there also and they said to him, "Are you not, too, one of his disciples?"

He denied it and said, "I am not."

Then one of the high priest's servants and a kinsman to the one whose ear Peter had cut off said, "Did I not see you in the garden with him?"

Peter then denied again and immediately the cock crew.

Then the Lord turned and looked at Peter and Peter remembered the words of Jesus, "Before the cock crows, you will deny me three times." And Peter went out and wept bitterly.

## JUDAS HANGS HIMSELF

Then Judas, who had betrayed him, when he saw that Jesus was condemned, repented and brought the thirty pieces of silver back to the chief priests and elders, saying, "I have sinned in that I have betrayed innocent blood."

They said, "What is that to us? That is your affair."

Then he threw down the pieces of silver in the temple, and went out and hanged himself.

And the chief priests took the silver pieces and said, "It is not lawful for us to put them into the treasury, because it is the price of blood." They discussed it, and bought with the silver the potter's field, to bury strangers in. That is why that field has been called the Field of Blood until this day.

## THE TRIAL

When the morning came, all the chief priests and elders of the people planned together against Jesus, to put him to death. And when they had bound him, they led him away to the hall of judgment and delivered him to Pontius Pilate, the Roman governor. They themselves did not go into the judgment hall, lest they should be ceremonially defiled, for they wanted to eat the Passover supper.

So Pilate came out to them and said, "What charge do you bring against this man?"

They answered and said to him, "If he were not a wrongdoer, we would not have delivered him to you."

Then Pilate said to them, "Take him and judge him according to your law."

But the people said to him, "It is not lawful for us to put any man to death."

Pilate went back into the judgment hall and called Jesus to him, and said to him, "Are you the King of the Jews?"

Jesus said to him, "Are you asking this of yourself, or did others say this about me?"

Pilate said, "Your own nation and the chief priests have delivered you to me. What have you done?"

Jesus answered, "My kingdom is not of this world. If my kingdom were of this world, my servants would have fought against my being delivered to the people. No, my kingdom is elsewhere."

Then Pilate said to him, "Are you a king, then?"

Jesus answered, "You say I am a king. To this end was I born, and for this cause I came into the world, that I should testify to the truth. Everyone who is on the side of truth listens to my voice."

## PILATE GIVES WAY

And Pilate said to him, "What is truth?" Then Pilate went out again to the people and said to them, "I find in him no fault at all. But you have a custom, that I should release to you one prisoner at the Passover. Do you wish therefore that I release to you Jesus?"

The chief priests and elders persuaded the people that they should ask for a notable prisoner, Barabbas, and put Jesus to death.

So they all cried out saying, "Not this man, but Barabbas." Barabbas was a robber and a murderer.

As Pilate was sitting on the judgment seat, his wife sent a message to him, saying, "Have nothing to do with that just man; for I have suffered many things this day in a dream concerning him."

So Pilate asked them again, "Which of the two shall I release to you? Barabbas, or Jesus which is called Christ?" And they said, "Barabbas." So Pilate

said, "What shall I do then with Jesus that is called Christ?" And they all said, "Let him be crucified."

And the governor said, "Why? What evil has he done?" But they cried out all the more, saying, "Let him be crucified."

So Pilate, seeing that he could not prevail on them and that there was an uproar, took water and washed his hands before the multitude, saying, "I am innocent of the blood of this just person."

Then all the people answered and said, "Let his blood be on us, and on our children."

And the voices of them and of the chief priests prevailed. And Pilate gave sentence that it should be as they required.

And he released Barabbas to them, and delivered Jesus to be crucified.

Then the soldiers of the governor took Jesus into the common hall and brought to him a band of soldiers. They stripped him and put on him a scarlet robe. Having braided a crown of thorns, they put it upon his head, and a reed in his right hand. They bowed the knee before him and mocked him saying, "Hail, King of the Jews!" They spat upon him and struck him with their hands. Taking the reed, they struck him upon the head. And after they had mocked him, they took the robe off him and put his own clothes on him. Then they led him away to crucify him.

# THE CRUCIFIXION

hey took Jesus and led him away; and he, bearing his cross, went forth to a place called the Place of a Skull, which is called in Hebrew Golgotha.

And as they led him along, they laid hold on one Simon, a Cyrenian, coming from the country, and they laid the cross on him that he might carry it, behind Jesus.

And there followed him a great group of people, and of women, bewailing him and lamenting him.

But Jesus turned to them and said, "Daughters of Jerusalem, weep not for me, but weep for yourselves and your children. For the days are coming in which people shall say to the mountains, 'Fall on us!' and to the hills, 'Cover us!'"

There were also two others, criminals, led out with him to be put to death. And when they had come to the place, which is called the Skull or Golgotha, they crucified him there, with the two criminals, one on the right hand, the other on the left.

Then Jesus said:

"Father, forgive them, for they know not what they do."

## THE ROBE IS DIVIDED

And the soldiers, when they had crucified Jesus, took his garments, and divided them into four parts, one to each soldier. They took his robe too. Now the robe was without seams, woven from the top down. Therefore they said among themselves, "Let us not tear it, but let us draw lots for it, to see whose it shall be." This was in order that the scripture might be fulfilled which says,

*"They parted my clothing among them, and for my robe they did cast lots."*

All these things, therefore, the soldiers did.

Now close by the cross of Jesus stood his mother, and his mother's sister, Mary the wife of Cleophas, and Mary Magdalene.

When Jesus saw his mother and a disciple whom he loved standing by, he said to his mother, "Woman, behold your son."

Then he said to the disciple, "Behold your mother." And from that hour that disciple took her into his own home.

675

## THE CROWD MOCKS JESUS

People stood by watching him, and others who passed by shouted abuse at him, wagging their heads and saying, "If you are the Son of God, come down from the cross." And the chief priests and rulers did likewise, saying, "He saved others; himself he cannot save. If he be the King of Israel, let him now come down from the cross and we will believe him. He trusted in God; let him deliver him now, if he will have him; for he said 'I am the Son of God.'"

Now from noon until three in the afternoon there was darkness all over the land.

And at three Jesus cried with a loud voice, "My God, my God, why have you forsaken me?" Knowing that all things were now completed that the scriptures might be fulfilled, Jesus said, "I thirst." One who stood by, ran and

filled a sponge with vinegar. Putting it upon a lance he gave it to him to drink sticking it in his mouth and saying: "Let us see whether his God will come to save him."

Over Jesus' head was a sign written in letters of Greek, Latin and Hebrew, reading, "This is the King of the Jews."

And one of the criminals who were crucified with him scoffed at him, saying, "If you are Christ, save your-self and us." But the other rebuked him, saying, "Do you not fear God, seeing that you are also condemned? And we are here justly, for we receive the due return for our deeds, but this man has done nothing wrong."

And he said to Jesus, "Lord, remember me when you come into your kingdom."

And Jesus said to him, "Truly I tell you today you shall be with me in paradise."

## JESUS GIVES UP THE GHOST

The sun was darkened, and the veil of the temple was torn in two from top to bottom. The earth quaked, rocks split, and graves were opened.

And when Jesus had cried with a loud voice, he said, "Father, into your hands I commend my spirit." And after this, he said, "It is finished," and bowed his head and gave up the ghost.

Now when the captain of the guard saw the earthquake and all those things that were done, he praised God, saying, "Truly this man was the Son of God."

All the people who had come to watch the spectacle, seeing the things which were done, beat their breasts and went away.

And those who knew him, and the women who had followed him from Galilee stood afar off, watching these things.

## THE BODY IS BURIED

The people, that the bodies should not remain on the crosses on the sabbath day, asked Pilate that he have them taken away. But when the soldiers came to Jesus, one of them with a spear pierced his side and forthwith there came out blood and water.

When evening was come, behold, a disciple of Jesus, a rich man named Joseph of Arimathea came secretly to

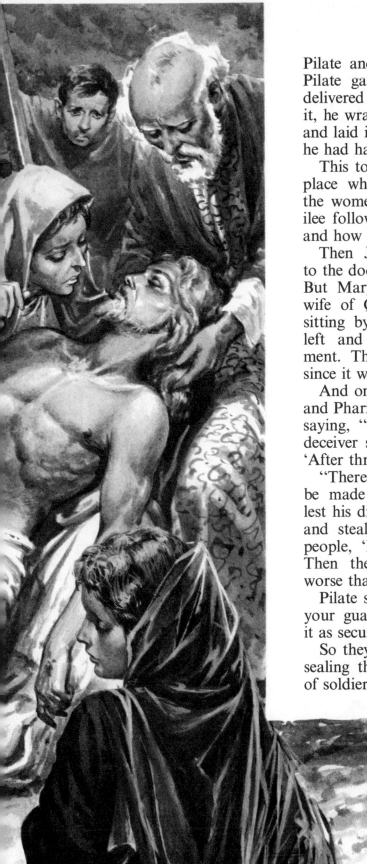

Pilate and begged the body of Jesus. Pilate gave orders that the body be delivered and when Joseph had taken it, he wrapped it in a clean linen cloth and laid it in his own new tomb which he had had hewn out of the rock.

This tomb was in a garden near the place where Jesus was crucified and the women who had come from Galilee followed along and saw the tomb and how his body was laid in it.

Then Joseph rolled a great stone to the door of the tomb, and departed. But Mary Magdalene and Mary the wife of Cleophas stayed for a while sitting by the tomb. Then they, too, left and prepared spices and ointment. They rested the following day since it was the sabbath.

And on the sabbath the chief priests and Pharisees went in a body to Pilate, saying, "Sir, we remember what that deceiver said, while he was still alive: 'After three days I will rise again.'

"Therefore command that the tomb be made secure until the third day, lest his disciples should come by night and steal him away, and say to the people, 'He is risen from the dead.' Then the final deception would be worse than the first."

Pilate said to them, "You may have your guard. Go your way and make it as secure as you can."

So they went and secured the tomb, sealing the stone and setting a guard of soldiers over it.

# THE RESURRECTION

AT the end of the sabbath, as it began to dawn on the first day of the week, Mary Magdalene and Mary the wife of Cleophas came to see the tomb. And, behold, there was a great earthquake, for the angel of the Lord descended from heaven and came back and rolled the stone from the entrance, and sat on it. His face was like lightning and his garments were white as snow.

For fear of him, the guards trembled and fainted away as if they were dead men. But the angel spoke to the women and said, "Fear not. For I know that you seek Jesus, who was crucified. He is not here, for he has risen, as he said. Come, see the place where the Lord lay.

"And now go quickly and tell his disciples that he has risen from the dead, for, behold, he goes ahead of you into Galilee, where you shall see him. There, I have told you."

They departed quickly from the tomb with fear and great joy, and ran to bring word to his disciples. And as they went to tell them, Jesus met them, saying, "All hail." And they came and held him by the feet and worshiped him.

Then Jesus said to them, "Be not afraid. Go and tell my brothers to go into Galilee, and there they shall see me."

## THE APPEARANCE
## TO THE DISCIPLES

On that same day, two of his disciples went to a village called Emmaus which was about seven miles from Jerusalem. They talked together about all these things which had happened. And it came to pass that while they discussed and reasoned together, Jesus himself came near and went with them. But they did not recognize him.

He said to them, "What manner of conversation is this that you make, one to another, as you walk and are so sad?"

One of them, whose name was Cleophas, answered, "Are you a stranger in Jerusalem? Have you not heard of the things that have come to pass there in these days?"

Jesus said to them, "What things?"

They said, "Concerning Jesus of Nazareth, who was a prophet mighty in deed and word before God and all the people, and how the chief priests and our rulers delivered him to be condemned to death and have crucified him. We had hoped that he was the man who would lead Israel.

"Today is the third day since these things were done, and certain women astonished us by telling us about how they went to the tomb where he was buried and had a vision of angels, who said that he was alive.

"Certain of our company went to the tomb, and found it was as the women had said, but they did not see him."

Then Jesus said to them, "O fools, and slow of heart to believe all that the prophets have spoken." And beginning at Moses and all the prophets, he explained to them the things in all the scriptures concerning himself.

And they drew near to the village where they were going and Jesus was going to walk on, but they stopped him, saying, "Stay with us, for it is toward evening and the day is far spent." So he went in and remained with them.

## THE BREAKING OF BREAD

As he sat eating with them, he took bread and blessed it and broke it, and gave it to them. Then their eyes were opened, and they knew him. But he had vanished out of their sight. Then they said to one another, "Did not our hearts burn within us while he talked with us on the road, and while he explained to us the scriptures?"

And they returned to Jerusalem in the same hour and found the eleven gathered together and they said, "The Lord is risen indeed, and has appeared to Simon." They told what things were done on the way to Emmaus and how he became known to them in breaking the bread.

## THE TAKING OF FOOD

As they thus spoke, Jesus himself stood in the midst of them and said to them, "Peace be unto you."

But they were terrified and much afraid and supposed that they had seen a spirit.

And he said to them, "Why are you troubled? And why do thoughts arise in your hearts? Behold my hands and my feet; that it is I myself. Handle me and see. For a spirit does not have flesh and bones, as you see me have."

And when he had thus spoken, he showed them his hands and his feet.

And while they still did not believe for joy, and wondered, he said to them, "Have you here any food?" And they gave him a piece of a broiled fish and of a honeycomb. And he took it, and did eat before them.

Then he said to them, "These are the words which I spoke to you while I was still with you, that all things must be done that were written in the law of Moses and in the Prophets and in the Psalms concerning me."

He opened their minds so that they might understand the scriptures, and said, "Thus it is written that it was necessary for Christ to suffer and to rise from the dead on the third day, and that repentance and forgiveness of sins should be preached in his name among all nations, beginning at Jerusalem. And you are witnesses of these things."

## THOMAS DOUBTS

But Thomas, one of the twelve, called Didymus (the Twin), was not with them when Jesus came. The disciples therefore said to him, "We have seen the Lord." But he said to them, "Unless I see in his hands the print of the nails, and put my finger into the print of the nails, and thrust my hand into his side, I will not believe."

After eight days, when the disciples were again in the room, and Thomas was with them, Jesus came to them, though the doors were shut, and stood among them and said, "Peace be unto you."

Then he said to Thomas, "Reach out your finger and touch my hands, and reach your hand here and thrust it into my side, and do not be faithless, but believe."

Thomas answered and said to him, "My Lord and my God."

Jesus said to him, "Thomas, because you have seen me you have believed. Blessed are they who have not seen, yet have believed."

## AT THE SEA OF TIBERIAS

After these things, Jesus showed himself again to his disciples at the sea of Tiberias. There were together Simon Peter and Thomas called Didymus and Nathanael of Cana, and the sons of Zebedee, and two others of his disciples.

Simon Peter said to them, "I go afishing." They said to him, "We also go with you." So they went forth and entered a boat immediately. They fished all night long and still caught nothing.

When the morning came, Jesus stood on the shore, but the disciples did not know that it was Jesus. He said to them, "Children, have you any food?"

"No," they answered him.

Then he said to them, "Cast your net on the right side of the boat and you will find fish." They cast therefore and they were not able to draw the net for the catch of fish. Therefore John, the disciple whom Jesus loved, said to Peter, "It is the Lord." And when Simon Peter heard that it was the Lord, he wrapped his fisher's coat round him (for he was naked), and cast himself into the sea.

The other disciples came in a little boat, for they were not far from land, and they dragged the net filled with fish. As soon as they had come to land, they saw a fire of coals there and fish laid on it, and some bread.

Jesus said to them, "Bring the fish that you have caught." Simon Peter went and pulled the net to land, full of great fishes, one hundred and fifty-three of them. And although there were so many, the net was not broken.

Jesus said to them, "Come and dine." And knowing that it was the Lord, none of them dared to ask him, "Who are you?"

So Jesus took the bread that was lying there and gave it to them and the fish likewise.

This was the third time that Jesus showed himself to his disciples after he had risen from the dead.

## JESUS ASCENDS INTO HEAVEN

Jesus appeared to his disciples for forty days, speaking of things concerning the kingdom of God. And while he was with them he commanded them not to leave Jerusalem, but to wait there for a promise from the Father. He said:

"For John truly baptized with water, but you shall be baptized with the Holy Spirit not many days from now. You shall receive power after the Holy Spirit has come upon you. You shall be witnesses for me in Jerusalem, and in all Judea, and in Samaria, and to the outermost parts of the earth."

Then Jesus led his disciples out as far as Bethany, and he lifted up his hands and blessed them. And while they looked on, he was taken up and a cloud received him out of their sight.

While they looked steadily toward heaven as he went up, behold, two men stood beside them in white robes and said to them, "You men of Galilee, why do you stand gazing up into heaven? This same Jesus who was taken up from you into heaven shall come again in the same way as you have seen him go."

And they worshiped him, and returned to Jerusalem with great joy, and were continually in the temple praising and blessing God.

# ILLUSTRATED GLOSSARY

### "Are you not one of this man's disciples?" (p. 671)

The servants knew that most of Jesus' apostles were from Galilee, so they were suspicious of Peter because he spoke in a Galilean dialect.

### Barabbas (p. 672)

Barabbas was a rebel who wanted to expel the Roman overlords from Palestine. He was involved in a revolt in Jerusalem against the Roman authorities. During the disturbance people were killed and Barabbas and other rebels were arrested.

### Beat their breasts (p. 678)

People beat their breasts, actually tapping lightly near the heart, as a sign of sorrow and repentance. This showed that the onlookers were genuinely sorry that Jesus had been crucified and that some of them recognized him as the Son of God.

### Bethphage (p. 652)

Bethphage, a small town outside of Jerusalem, was located on the eastern slope of the Mount of Olives.

### Captain of the guard (p. 678)

This captain of the guard, who witnessed the crucifixion of Jesus, was a Roman centurion.

### Cedron (p. 669)

The brook Cedron, sometimes called Kidron, is dry most of the year and forms a narrow valley. It begins about a mile north of Jerusalem and continues to the Dead Sea. At one point Cedron forms a canyon 100 feet wide and 400 feet deep.

### Ceremonially defiled (p. 672)

The elders were taking precautions against being defiled, or being made spiritually unclean, because the Passover was approaching. Such defilement would have prevented them from taking part in the Passover feast, or Seder.

Contact with Gentiles was a possible cause of defilement, and so the elders did not want to be in the same room with the Roman governor, officials, and soldiers.

### The cock will not crow (p. 668)

A cock is a rooster, or male chicken. The chickens kept in Palestine were red jungle fowls of Asia. The handsome birds were brightly colored, and could fly, unlike today's barnyard fowls.

Cocks usually crowed three times at night: about midnight, again at about 4 A.M., and again at sunrise. They crowed so punctually that people used them to help tell time. It was

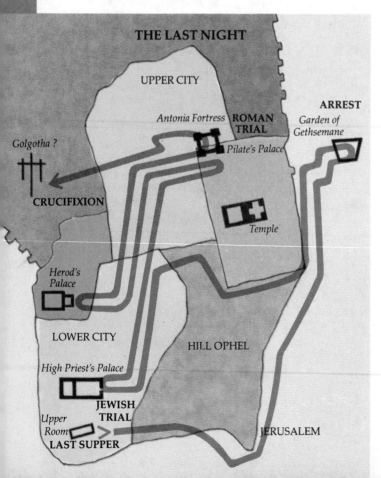

THE LAST NIGHT

UPPER CITY

Antonia Fortress  ROMAN TRIAL

ARREST
Garden of Gethsemane

Golgotha ?

Pilate's Palace

CRUCIFIXION

Temple

Herod's Palace

LOWER CITY

HILL OPHEL

High Priest's Palace

JEWISH TRIAL

Upper Room

LAST SUPPER

JERUSALEM

probably the midnight crowing that led Peter to recall Jesus' words: "The cock will not crow before you have denied me three times."

## Colt (p. 652)

A colt is a young male animal of the horse family. Jesus rode into Jerusalem on a colt that was a young ass or donkey.

## Crown of thorns (p. 674)

Because there were so many wild thorn plants growing in Palestine, no one can be sure which one was used to make the cruel crown of thorns Jesus was made to wear. Many believe it was the Jerusalem thorn, which grew wild in and around Jerusalem. This plant was not as stiff as some thorns, and the branches could have been twisted into a crown.

## A Disciple whom he loved (p. 675)

John used the words "a disciple whom Jesus loved" to describe himself in his Gospel.

## Doves (p. 654)

Doves are closely related to pigeons, but are slightly smaller and are paler in color. Both birds were common in Palestine.

The pigeon and the dove are swift fliers. They can take off very quickly and keep up their speed for long distances. Pigeons stayed in Palestine all year, but doves wintered in Africa.

## The Eleven (p.684)

"The Eleven" means the eleven apostles who remained after Judas Iscariot killed himself in despair because he had betrayed Jesus. Later, the eleven remaining apostles chose lots to decide between two men to take the place of Judas. The lot fell to a man named Matthias.

## Emmaus (p. 680)

The Bible tells us Emmaus was seven miles from Jerusalem, but its exact location is not known. This town played an important role in Jewish history.

In the 2nd century B.C., the Seleucids, who were occupying Jerusalem and had plundered the temple, planned to take all of Judah. Their army marched to Emmaus and camped nearby.

The Jews were determined to overthrow their enemy because Antiochus Epiphanes had forbidden the Jews to practice their religion and had defiled the temple. A brave leader, Judas Maccabeus, son of the equally brave Mattathias, met the Seleucids at Emmaus and defeated them. The Jews then recaptured Jerusalem, and the temple was purified. The happy celebration that followed is repeated each year as Chanukah, the Feast of Dedication.

## Fruit of the vine (p. 668)

"The fruit of the vine" meant wine, since grapes, which are made into wine, grow on vines.

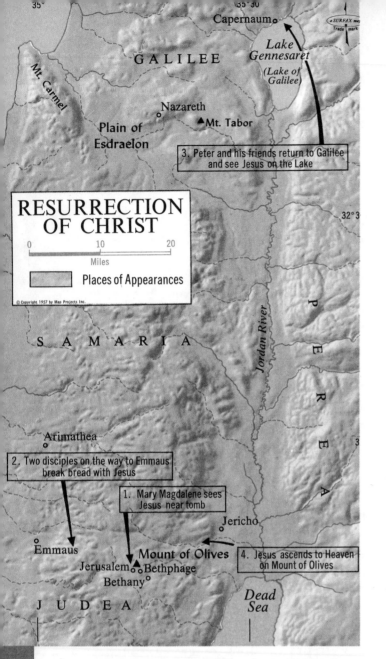

## RESURRECTION OF CHRIST

0    10    20
Miles

Places of Appearances

© Copyright 1957 by Map Projects Inc.

Mt. Carmel

GALILEE

Lake Gennesaret
(Lake of Galilee)

Capernaum

Nazareth

▲Mt. Tabor

Plain of Esdraelon

3. Peter and his friends return to Galilee and see Jesus on the Lake

S A M A R I A

Jordan River

P E R E A

32°3

Arimathea

2. Two disciples on the way to Emmaus break bread with Jesus

1. Mary Magdalene sees Jesus near tomb

Jericho

Emmaus

Mount of Olives

Jerusalem
Bethphage
Bethany

4. Jesus ascends to Heaven on Mount of Olives

J U D E A

Dead Sea

### The Garden of Gethsemane (p. 669)

Gethsemane was not only a garden, but was also a small orchard of olive trees. It was called Gethsemane, which meant oil press in Aramaic, because olives were gathered and the oil was pressed from them right in the garden.

The Garden of Gethsemane lay outside the east gate of Jerusalem about three-fourths of a mile from the city, on the western slope of the Mount of Olives.

### "Give therefore to Caesar the things which are Caesar's and to God the things which are God's" (p. 656)

Throughout history, Christians have turned to this passage to understand how Jesus intended them to live in relation to their government.

### Honeycomb (p. 684)

Honeycombs are wax structures made by bees for storing honey, pollen, and eggs. The combs are divided into small six-sided cells that are arranged side by side. In some cells, the bees store the honey and the pollen that are their food. In others, the queen bee lays her eggs. The eggs remain in the cells where they hatch and the bees grow to maturity.

When Jesus asked his apostles for food, they gave him a comb containing honey.

### Hosanna to the Son of David (p. 654)

"Hosanna to the Son of David" was a cry used as a cheer or applause. Hosanna is from Hebrew words that mean "save us, we pray." Jesus was called the Son of David because he came from the family of King David.

### Joseph of Arimathea (p. 678)

Joseph of Arimathea was a member of the Sanhedrin, but it is believed that he was not present when Jesus was questioned by Caiaphas.

The location of Joseph's home town, where he took Jesus' body, is not known for certain.

694

## Lamps (p. 660)

The lamps most commonly used at that time looked like pottery saucers. The edge of one side was pinched to make a lip, like that on a small cream pitcher. A wick made of hemp or flax string lay on the lip, with one end resting in the oil in the saucer. Olive oil was usually burned, but sometimes animal fat was used.

## Let this cup pass from me (p. 669)

Jesus knew that great suffering was in store for him. In the Garden of Gethsemane, he prayed to God to spare him. "This cup" meant the crucifixion and the agony that would go with it.

## A Man carrying a pitcher of water (p. 664)

The apostles were instructed to look for a man carrying a pitcher of water. They would have had no trouble finding such a man, because in those days it was women who carried water from the wells, and few men did such work.

## Moneychanger (p. 654)

Jews coming from distant lands to Jerusalem had to pay the temple tax. This tax was required by Mosaic Law of all male Jews who were twenty years of age or older. Because the tax had to be paid in shekels, foreigners had to change their money into the coins of Palestine. This service was performed by moneychangers who charged their customers a fee that was sometimes excessive.

## Mount of Olives (p. 652)

The Mount of Olives, one of a range of hills near Jerusalem, was opposite the city's eastern wall. Its top was 200 feet higher than Jerusalem, and from it one had a fine view of the city.

The Mount of Olives was named for the many old olive trees that grew on its slopes. The trees made the hill a pleasant, shady place on hot, sunny days.

## Nathanael of Cana (p. 686)

Nathanael of Cana is possibly the same man as the apostle Bartholomew. Matthew, Mark, and Luke include Bartholomew with the other apostles in their Gospels. Nowhere do they mention an apostle named Nathanael. John mentions Nathanael in his Gospel, but never speaks of Bartholomew. In this Gospel, too, Nathanael is always in the company of other apostles.

Jesus was speaking of Nathanael when he said: "Behold an Israelite without guile." He meant that Nathanael was a simple and honest man.

## Not on the feast (p. 663)

The feast was Passover, celebrated in memory of the Israelites' escape from slavery in Egypt. Those who wished to kill Jesus feared that the Passover would stir up emotions that might lead the people to riot against their Roman rulers.

## Passover feast (p. 664)

The Passover feast, or Seder, was eaten after sunset on the first evening of the Passover. On that night, Jesus and his apostles had planned to eat the holiday meal.

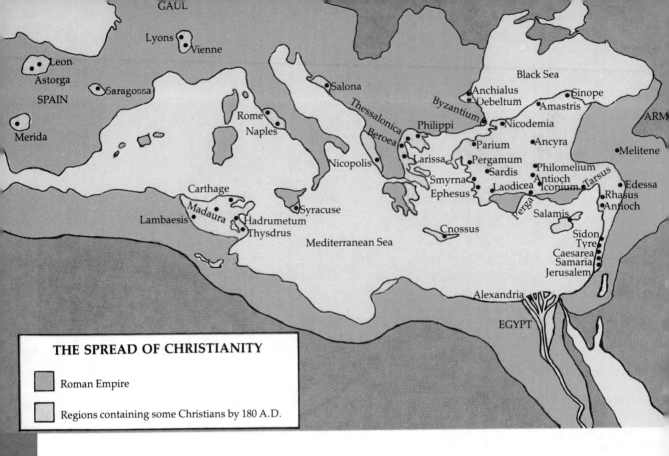

GAUL

Lyons• •Vienne

Leon•
Astorga •
SPAIN

•Saragossa

Merida •

Rome •
Naples •

Carthage •

Madaura •
Lambaesis • Hadrumetum
Thysdrus

Salona •

Thessalonica
Beroea •
Nicopolis •
Larissa •

Syracuse •

Black Sea
Anchialus •
Debeltum •
Byzantium •
Philippi •
Parium •
Pergamum •
Sardis •
Smyrna • Laodicea • Antioch
Ephesus • Iconium •
Perga
Salamis •

Sinope •
Amastris •
Nicodemia •
Ancyra •
Philomelium •
Tarsus
Edessa •
Rhasus •
Antioch •

ARM

Melitene •

Cnossus •

Sidon
Tyre •
Caesarea •
Samaria •
Jerusalem •

Mediterranean Sea

Alexandria •

EGYPT

### THE SPREAD OF CHRISTIANITY

☐ Roman Empire

☐ Regions containing some Christians by 180 A.D.

### Place of a skull (p. 674)

The hill near Jerusalem where Jesus was crucified was called the Skull because of its shape. It is known by two other names, both meaning skull: "Calvary," from the Latin language, and "Golgotha," from the Aramaic.

### Potter's field (p. 672)

Potters, who molded clay into dishes, pots, lamps, and other objects, placed their pottery in sunny fields to dry. In ancient cities these so-called potter's fields were often used as burial places. The potter's field that was bought with Judas' thirty silver pieces was located outside Jerusalem. It was used as a burial place for strangers. Today the term potter's field is used for any place where strangers and paupers are buried.

### Prepared spices and ointment (p. 679)

It was the Jews' custom for women to anoint a body with fragrant ointments and to wrap it with cloths and spices before it was buried. Because Jesus' body was taken down from the cross near the end of the day, and sundown marked the beginning of the Sabbath, Jesus' women friends didn't have enough time to make all the burial preparations.

In their homes, before the sun set, they made an ointment of olive oil and fragrant herbs and chose pleasant-smelling herbs to put in the shroud. At dawn of the first day of the week, when the Sabbath ended, the women hurried back to the tomb, intending to finish preparing Jesus' body.

### Sea of Tiberias (p. 686)

This was another name for the Sea of Galilee.

### Simon, a Cyrenian (p. 674)

Simon, who helped carry Jesus' cross, was probably a man of Cyrene, a Greek city in North Africa. Many Jews

696

had settled there in the 3rd century B.C. Simon had apparently returned at some time to work in Palestine. Perhaps he wanted his sons, Rufus and Alexander, to live in their ancestral country. It is also possible that, like many Jews, he was on a visit to Jerusalem to celebrate the Passover.

## Sons of Zebedee (p. 686)

The sons of Zebedee were the apostles James and John. Zebedee and his sons were fishermen on the Sea of Galilee.

At that time, people did not have last names. Since people often had the same names, men were frequently identified by their father's name as well as their own. Thus James and John were called the sons of Zebedee. "Bar" meant "son of," and it preceded such Jewish names as Bartholomew, Barabbas, and Barnabas.

Sometimes the town of birth was included in a person's name, as in Simon the Cyrenian and Joseph of Arimathea.

## Temple of God (p. 654)

This was the temple built by Herod the Great. Started in 20 B.C., the main building was quickly finished, but the buildings around it were not completed until 64 A.D. and work was still being done during Jesus' time. The temple was destroyed in 70 A.D. by the Romans.

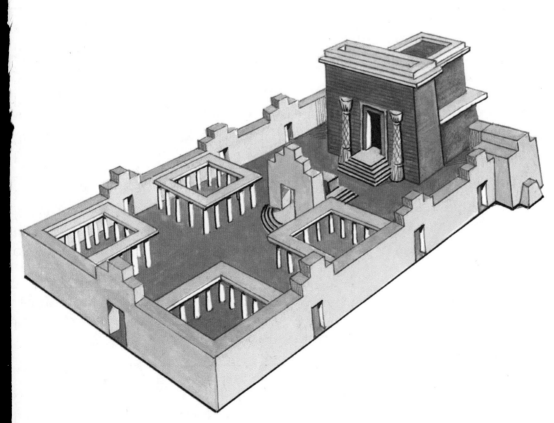

A reconstruction of King Herod's Temple.

A garden tomb was usually built into the side of a hill.

## Tomb (p. 679)

A tomb is a chamber where a corpse is buried. In Palestine, tombs were usually caves or rooms cut into rock. The bodies were laid inside the tomb on stone couches. A round stone was rolled in a groove to close the entrance to the tomb.

Each family had its own tomb, sometimes in a cemetery, often in a garden. Those who could not afford a tomb buried their dead in the ground. Strangers were buried in a potter's field. (See Potter's field.)

## Treasury (p. 656)

The treasury was thirteen boxes that were kept in the temple courtyard. People dropped their offerings and their temple taxes, which was a half-shekel a year from every Jewish man, in the boxes. The Temple of Herod also had a room called a treasury where precious objects were kept.

## Tribute to Caesar (p. 656)

The tribute to Caesar was the tax the Jews had to pay to the Roman government. Such taxes were numerous and the Jews resented these taxes imposed by a foreign ruler. Everyone had to pay a personal tax and then a tax on property. The people who lived in Jerusalem had to pay a tax on their homes as well.

## Trimmed their lamps (p. 660)

To trim a lamp meant to prepare it to give a good light. The basin of the lamp (see Lamp) was filled with olive oil and the wick was cut to the proper length and positioned so it would draw up the oil.

## Veil of the temple (p. 678)

The veil of the temple was a curtain that hung from golden hooks before the Holy of Holies where the Ark of the Covenant was kept. The Old Testament specified that the veil be made of linen and woolen cloth, and that it be blue, purple, and scarlet and embroidered with gold thread.

## You shall be witnesses for me (p. 687)

A witness is a person who knows about an event because he saw or heard it happen. The witnesses to Jesus were the disciples who had seen his miracles and heard his words. When Jesus said: "You shall be witnesses for me . . . to the outermost parts of the earth," he was telling his disciples to be missionaries and carry his message to all the people of the world.

# HOW ARCHEOLOGISTS STUDY BIBLICAL TOWNS

Archeologists who excavate, or dig up, sites of biblical towns and cities have taught us a great deal about how people lived in ancient times. These highly trained men and women investigate the sites where the towns were situated. They unearth pieces of pottery, metal objects, and the ruins of buildings for studying and dating.

Often the biblical towns are located on sites where towns have been destroyed and rebuilt many times. The earliest settlers built on ground-level, but when the towns were re-built, the ashes and rubble of the previous town were not cleared away. New buildings were simply erected on top of the ruins. Because of this, the towns eventually were sitting on top of a hill, called a tell, which could be as high as 90 feet.

Archeologists showed, for instance, that the ancient city of Megiddo had a very long history. Twenty separate sets of ruins were discovered between layers of ash and debris on its site. From this evidence, archeologists proved that the city must have been destroyed and rebuilt nineteen times

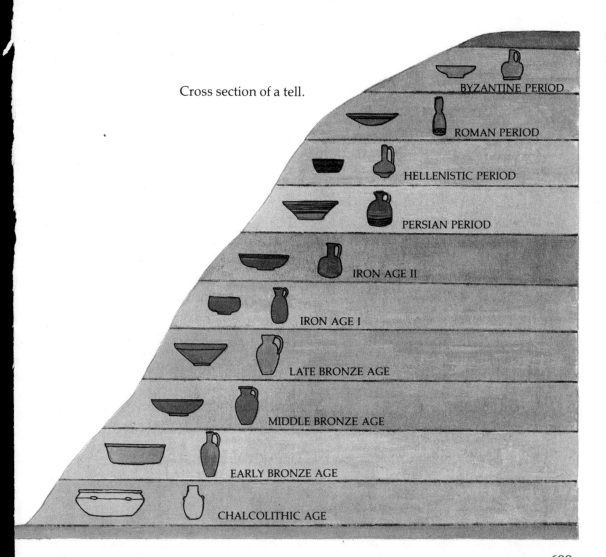

Cross section of a tell.

BYZANTINE PERIOD

ROMAN PERIOD

HELLENISTIC PERIOD

PERSIAN PERIOD

IRON AGE II

IRON AGE I

LATE BRONZE AGE

MIDDLE BRONZE AGE

EARLY BRONZE AGE

CHALCOLITHIC AGE

since about 3500 B.C. Megiddo occupied a key pass between the coastal plain of Sharon and the Plain of Jezreel. It was a prize that was fought for again and again by the different peoples who occupied Palestine, as the excavations prove.

When archeologists excavate on such a mound, they carefully clear the tell, layer by layer, and sift through the dirt in search of relics. Sometimes they cut trenches, but only at carefully selected spots. By working this way, they unearth objects from only one town or time period at a time. The excavators must be very careful to avoid mixing any relics from different layers, or their studies will be confusing and inaccurate.

Usually the top of the mound represents the site of a modern Turkish or Arab town. Beneath that may be found ruins from the time of the Crusades, and beneath those may be ruins of the Byzantine period. Deeper may be relics of the Roman, Maccabean, Hellenistic, Persian, Babylonian, and Israelite eras. Often traces dating as far back as the Canaanite occupations can be found.

Eventually the archeologists reach bedrock or virgin soil at the site. When this happens they know they have dated the beginning of human occupation of that particular location.

Many things are unearthed in each layer of the tell. Bits of broken pots, statues, jewelry, tools, weapons, and objects used in everyday life are discovered. From these things, arche-ologists can date the layer and tell a great deal about the way the people lived.

Pottery is especially important for determining a date. Scientists look at the shape of the handles, the kind of clay and paint used, and the way the pottery was fired, or baked. These clues tell a scientist when the piece was made. By dating the pottery, they can date the layer where it was found and establish the general history of the site.

Archeologists also date layers by studying the ruins of walls and buildings. Different tools and methods of cutting were used in different periods. Archeologists have been able to unearth and identify parts of King Saul's fortress at Gibeah, and ancient walls of the city of Jerusalem. Some of these walls date back to the Canaanite period. Other findings represent repairs or additions to the walls made by King Saul and King David. Still other findings were walls built during Jesus' time. These studies have confirmed the biblical account of David's conquest of the city from the Jebusites.

By studying such ancient walls and ruined buildings, the archeologists can determine how a city was laid out. They can locate the streets and the markets. Then they can build models or make drawings to show how these ancient cities of Palestine might have looked. Thanks to archeologists' discoveries, we know a great deal today about how people lived and worked during biblical times.

# NEW TESTAMENT HISTORY

## ROME

## PALESTINE

### — 100 B.C. —

**Roman Rule Over Palestine**
  **63 B.C.-A.D. 135**
POMPEY'S ENTRANCE INTO JERUSALEM 63 B.C.
ASSASSINATION OF JULIUS CAESAR 44 B.C.
BATTLE OF ACTIUM 31 B.C.
*Caesar Augustus* 29 B.C.-A.D. 14

*Alexander Jannaeus* 103-76 B.C.
*Alexandra* 76-67 B.C.
*Aristobulus* II 67-63 B.C.
POMPEY'S ENTRANCE INTO JERUSALEM 63 B.C.
*Hyrcanus* II 63-40 B.C.
JERUSALEM TAKEN BY PARTHIANS 40 B.C.
*Herod the Great* 37-4 B.C.
BIRTH OF JESUS 6 B.C.
*Archelaus* 4 B.C.-A.D. 6

### — A.D. —

*Tiberius Caesar* A.D. 14-37
MINISTRY OF JESUS A.D. 28-29
DEATH OF JESUS A.D. 29
MARTYRDOM OF STEPHEN AND
  CONVERSION OF SAUL A.D. 35
*Caligula* A.D. 37-41
BARNABAS AND SAUL, ANTIOCH AND
  JERUSALEM A.D. 41-42
PERSECUTION OF HEROD AGRIPPA I A.D. 44
PAUL'S FIRST JOURNEY, COUNCIL
  AT JERUSALEM A.D. 46-47

*Herod Antipas* 4 B.C.-A.D. 34
**Roman Procurators in Palestine**
  **6 B.C.-A.D. 37**
*Philip* 4 B.C.-A.D. 37
*Pontius Pilate* A.D. 27-37

### — A.D. 50 —

I-II *Thessalonians*
*Galatians*
I-II *Corinthians*
*Romans, Philippians*
*Colossians, Philemon*
*Mark*
I-II *Timothy*
*Titus*
*Luke, Acts*
*Matthew, James*
*John, Hebrews*
I *John*
*Revelation*
I-III *John*
*Peter, Jude*

*Claudius* A.D. 41-54
PAUL'S SECOND JOURNEY A.D. 48-51

PAUL'S THIRD JOURNEY A.D. 52-57
*Nero* A.D. 54-68
IMPRISONMENT OF PAUL A.D. 57-62
PERSECUTION OF NERO A.D. 64
*Galba, Otto, Vitellius* A.D. 68-69
*Vespasian,* A.D. 69-79
*Titus* A.D. 79-81
*Domitian* A.D. 81-96
*Nerva* A.D. 96-98

JEWISH REVOLT A.D. 66-70
FALL OF JERUSALEM A.D. 70
DESTRUCTION OF THE TEMPLE
  A.D. 70

### — A.D. 100 —

I *Peter*
*End of New Testament*

*Trajan* 98-117
*Hadrian* 117-138
REVOLT OF BAR-COCHBA 132-135

### — A.D. 135 —